VERSE OR PERVERSE

Poetry by Ralph D. Katherman

Illustrations by Hollis Daniel

StoryArtsMedia

VERSE OR PERVERSE
Text Copyright © 2015 Ralph D. Katherman

Original Illustrations Copyright © 2015 Hollis Daniel

Roy Lichtenstein's *Live Ammo*, Paul Stephenson's *The Wounded Indian*,
Gustave Dore's *The Neophyte*, Pierre Auguste Renoir's *Daughters of Durand-Ruel*,
and Franz Kline's *Hot Jazz* used with permission of the Chrysler Museum, Norfolk, VA.
Arshile Gorky's *Still Life* used with permission of the Philadelphia Museum of Art.
Salvador Dali's *The Persistence of Memory* used with permission of MOMA.

Cover and Interior Design by Joseph Daniel

ISBN: 978-0-9863741-3-5
Library of Congress Control Number: 2015932530

No part of this book may be reproduced or transmitted in any form
or by any means, electronic or mechanical, including photocopying,
recording, or by any information storage and retrieval system,
without written permission from the publisher.

All rights reserved.

Published by Story Arts Media
PO Box 1230, Boulder, CO 80306
www.storyartsmedia.com

For Helen

The greatest gift I know is an act of love,
For whether giver or receiver be, it can make you whole
'Tis more lovely than the stars in a summer sky above
And becomes a part of both giver and receiver's soul.

At a poetry seminar several years ago, the participants were required to read a poem on the subject of how a poem should be read with the intent of finding its true meaning beyond its words and suggested that a poem was not valid unless it was so cloaked in metaphor that the reader couldn't understand it. Since I believe that poetry is also a proper vehicle for the expression of emotion, etc. without the use of metaphor and is still valid, I was provoked by the above mentioned poem to write this following poem which, I believe, accurately expresses my view of poetry and will give you a preview of what you might encounter herein should you decide to read any further:

POETRY DEFROCKED

Some poems wear their words like a splendid robe
Beneath which, it is said, the reader must probe
To find some hidden meaning lurking there
As though those poems had on their underwear.
Now I find those poems' robes to be quite fair
Even though I can't see their underwear.
Other poems, though, wear a splendid word-woven robe
Beneath which there is no reason to probe
For, if beneath their robes you should dare to peek
All you'd see would be a bare, nude cheek,
But I deem these poems' robes to be no less fair
Just because they have no underwear.

Ralph D. Katherman
2007

Table of Contents

HUMOR

Animals, Nature & Science

OH THE WONDERFUL WORLD OF BIRDS 11
THE GNU 12
WHAT'S A RHINOCEROS? 12
THOSE DAMNED CATS 13
CATATONIC 14
WITH A HANK OF HAIR 15
WHAT'S IN A NAME? 15
PETA INVESTIGATES 16
FOOD CHAIN 16
ANIMAL TALES 17
OUT OF PLACE 18
THANKSGIVING 19
A GARDEN OF MY OWN 19
TWO STRANGE OLD BIRDS 20
SNOWFALL 20
MARCH INTO SPRING 20

The Arts

THE OPERA FROM HELL 22
OH HELL! DALI! 23
I'M OUT OF HERE 24
THE MASTICATION, REGURGITATION AND ENCAPSULATION OF SHAKESPEARE'S ROMEO AND JULIET 25
ROSES IN BLOOM 26
COLORS 27
ANTIGONE IN A NUTSHELL 28
WHO HAS THE LAST LAUGH NOW! 30
THE JAZZ SINGER 31
FEELINGS? 32
THEY'RE ALL ALIKE 33
THE CURTAIN DESCENDS 33

Age, Health & Lifestyle
THE PHYSICAL EXAM 35
TEN DAYS OUT OF MY GOLDEN YEARS 35
A WELL-BALANCED DIET 36
TROPHIES 37
HOUSE FOR SALE 37
PARADOX 38
HOPIN' 38
MEMORIES AND DREAMS 39
WHEN I'M GONE 39
LIFE'S SHORT – SO EAT DESSERT FIRST 39
THAT'S FOR CERTAIN 40
A SHOPPER'S LAMENT 40
THE ROAD MORE TRAVEL'D 40
SECRET GARDENS 41
MORNING 41
TEMPTATION VERSE 42
SHORT CIRCUITS 42
BALLS 42
WHEN TWO HEARTS COLLIDE 42
ETERNITY 43
THERE IS NO ART IN FAILURE:
AUTOBIOGRAPHY OF A LOSER 43
LIFE IS JUST A BOWL OF CHERRIES 44
A LIFE OF BIBLICAL IMPORT 44
DEATH DANCES ROUND MY BED AT NIGHT 44
A LITTLE LOVE FROM YOU 45
HAIKU! GESUNDHEIT! 46
WRINKLES 47

Travel & Holidays
A WEE BIT OF ENGLAND 49
OUTER BANKS 51
SAN FRANCISCO 52
THE BAH! HUMBUG! TREE 52
HAVE YOURSELF A FURRY LITTLE CHRISTMAS 53

SANTA'S RETIREMENT 53
A LETTER FROM SANTA 54
A SMOKY CHRISTMAS 55
I'M CANCELLING CHRISTMAS THIS YEAR 56
HALLOWEEN 58
RESOLUTIONS 59

HEARTBREAK
Love & Loss
CUPID'S GENTLE WOUND 63
THREE DARK NIGHTS 63
A FEW LINES WRITTEN ON ONE OF MY BETTER DAYS 64
THE LANDFILL OF YESTERDAYS 64
IN APRIL 65
CHASTITY 65
A LOVELY FLOW'R 66
LOVE IS A GAME 66
I'LL TELL YOU WHAT I'LL DO 67
THE GRASS IS ALWAYS GREENEST 68
OUR LOVE 68
ON ADDICTION 69
LIVIN' & LOVIN' 69
FAMILY LIFE 69
IN THE MATTER OF THE LORD VS. THE DEVIL 69
THE REAL TRUTH ABOUT THE BURDEN OF PROOF 70
STIMULUS ANTHEM! 70
THE NEW MEXICAN NATIONAL ANTHEM 71
WEEP NO MORE MY LADY 71
THE IRAQ WAR CHRONICLES 72
BY THE BLOOD OF OTHERS STAINED 72
WOUNDED WORLD 73
DEAD END 74
A PLACE NOW DEAD 75

HUMOR

Animals, Nature & Science

OH, THE WONDERFUL WORLD OF BIRDS

The turkeys, the owls, the robins, the wrens,
The falcons, the terns, the roosters, the hens,
The egrets, the ducks, the magpies, the rails,
The warblers, the geese, the hawks and the quails.
    Oh, the wonderful world of birds!

Birds come in all sizes, shapes and colors,
Fly into O'Hare, Kennedy and Dulles
And with a strut or a prance, a song or a dance,
The males court their girls into romance
    Oh, the wonderful world of birds!

Nearly all birds have only one mate,
Monogamous, now isn't that great,
But to insure no drop in their population
They also have extra pair copulation.
    Oh, the wonderful world of birds!

For a bird there is no greater bliss
Than giving its mate a cloacal kiss.
To us, it doesn't make very much sense,
But for them it's very, very intense.
    Oh, the wonderful world of birds!

Birds, you know, don't have any bladder
And only a little more brain
And when they fly over they drop matter
That'll give your clothing a stain.
    Oh, the wonderful world of birds!

Male birds, they don't have any penis,
Now ain't that a terrible shame
They gave it up, strictly between us,
For an aerodynamic frame.
    Oh, the wonderful world of birds!

Bird's bones are really quite hollow
From the eagle right down to the swallow
Which when in flight makes them more buoyant
So, while flying they have more enjoyment.
      Oh, the wonderful world of birds!

Birds have a wonderful thing called a feather
Which keeps them safe through all sorts of weather
And they never get lost during flights between places
Which is more than we can say for our suitcases.
      Oh, the wonderful world of birds!

Where did I acquire all this avian knowledge?
If it's not accurate, I hope you won't scold me,
'Cause I didn't learn it at any school or college,
It's just something a little birdie once told me.
      Oh, the wonderful world of birds!

THE GNU

How old, I asked, is the wildebeest
The zookeeper said, "Why, he's twenty at least."
How surprised I was to have been told
That the gnu wasn't new, but really old.

WHAT'S A RHINOCEROS?

I'm gonna tell you something
That you'll probably think
Is corny.

I believe a rhinoceros
Is a hippopotamus
That's horny.

THOSE DAMNED CATS

I wake each morn to start a brand new day,
To find I have two obstacles in my way.
        Those damned cats!

I fix my breakfast, just a little something stable,
Then find I can't eat it sitting at a table.
        Those damned cats!

I move around my place, go from room to room
But fear each step, I'll trip, fall down, go boom.
        Those damned cats!

I sit at my computer to retrieve and read e-mail,
But before I can read it, it's all gone stale.
        Those damned cats!

I wash up all my dirty clothes, then try to fold,
But before I finish, I'll be way, way past old.
        Those damned cats!

I try to clean up all the counters in my kitchen,
But all I ever get done is some real loud bitchin'.
        Those damned cats!

I fix myself an evening meal upon which to sup,
But like all my meals, have to eat it standing up.
        Those damned cats!

I go to bed at night beneath my covers deep,
But it's seldom that I get a chance to sleep.
        Those damned cats!

Now, if I were a God with the power to compel,
Those two I'd quickly judge, then send straight to hell.
        Those damned cats!

And, as for the one who brought them here to start,
I should, but won't, drive a dagger through her heart.
     Those damned cats!

CATATONIC

If a cat poops on your carpet, is that a catastrophe as well as a cat-ass-trophy?

If you wish to have your cat groomed, do you have to send it to the catacombs?

If your cat wished to go sailing, would it do so on a catamaran?

If your cat wanted to do some shopping, would it use a Sears catalogue?

If your cat is meowing loudly, is it caterwauling?

If your cat was religious, would it be Catholic?

If your cat was Catholic, would it know its catechism?

If your car isn't running properly, is something wrong with its catalytic converter?

If you got rid of your cat, would that be cathartic?

To get rid of my cat, do I have to move to Piscataway, N.J.?

In asking these questions, was I being catachrestic?

WITH A HANK OF HAIR
Dedicated to Professor Joseph C. Daniel

It's really amazing what scientists can make today in a jar,
But do you think, perhaps, they go a little too far?
By use of in vitro or artificial insemination, maybe,
They can, without any intercourse, make you a baby.

With a gene splice here and, perhaps, another one there,
They can change what should have been an apple into a pear.
With a hank of my hair or a small piece of my bone
They can reproduce me in the form of a clone.

Extinct species, dead for at least an eternity,
They can recreate from a cell without a trace of paternity.
With a transplanted gene and a swirl and a swish,
They can grow human organs in a petri dish.

By altering a gene or, perhaps, two or three,
They can change an old plant into a new variety.
Now, are these acts within the bounds of propriety?
Will they really be of benefit to our society?

Though, I think the answer to these questions is certainly "Yes"
I'm afraid I must also stand up and readily confess
That life was a lot easier to understand, for me,
When, as the poet then put it, only God could make a tree.

WHAT'S IN A NAME?

This may make sense, but not very much,
A group of chicks is called a clutch.
And this is the truth, though it may sound odd,
That a group of seals is called a pod.
And I hope saying this won't get me in a jam,

But a group of whales is called a gam.
This, too, is true, so please don't haggle,
A group of geese is called a gaggle.
This is a fact, though it sounds absurd.
But a group of cattle is called a herd.
Here's another fact, so, please, take stock
A group of sheep is often called a flock.
And this, I know, is not just a crock,
A group of birds is also called a flock.
Now, try this one on for size, you will lovey
A small flock of birds is called a covey.
And here's one from which I cannot hide,
A large group of lions is called a pride.
And I know this, 'cause I'm no fool,
A group of fish is called a school
Now I'm gonna say this and not take it back,
That a group of wolves is called a pack.
Finally, this from experience, I can confirm,
A group of sharks is called a law firm.

PETA INVESTIGATES

PETA asked the cookie company this question.
To which it has not received a reply
To make one molasses cookie
How many moles have to die?

FOOD CHAIN

High in the sky, one summer day,
I watched an eagle circle its prey
And, while some may weep for the prey it sought
That eagle was doing only what it ought.

ANIMAL TALES

I'd rather be a bull frog
Than anything else I know
I'd live in a pond down in the bog
Where the water lilies grow
I'd sun all day on a sunken log
Just watching the marsh tide flow
Those warming rays all day long I'd soak
And when night came, I'd party 'til I'd croak!

I'd rather be a jack rabbit
Than anything else I know
Reproduction would be my habit
I'd have a million heirs or so.
I'd live out under a sky of blue
Where carrots and cabbages grow
Then I'd just do what all rabbits do
And watch my family grow and grow.

I'd rather be any elephant
Than anything else I know
And if I were, I'd pack my trunk
And a traveling I would go
But, maybe, if I were I wouldn't be amused
And 'stead a traveling, just pace to and fro
If I got my trunk and tail confused
And didn't know which way to go.

I'd rather be a rattlesnake
Than anything else I know
I'd live out in the canebrake
And be feared wherever I might go
Now this to you may sound sappy
But I want you to carefully listen,
All it would take then to make me happy
Would be a big pit to hiss in

I'd rather be a dragon
Than anything else I know
Then I'd have no need for braggin'
I could breathe fire on every so and so,
But I'll remain just as I am,
Not a word can sway me
For if I was a dragon,
St. George would come and slay me.

OUT OF PLACE

The spider hangs proudly on its web of silk
The baby suckles its mother's sweet, warm milk
The sand crab finds safety in its shady hole
The gold fish seems happy swimming in its bowl
The monkey swings from limb to limb with glee
Why do I feel that monkey's merely mocking me?

The cat can find contentment anywhere
The dog can find it in its master's chair
The rabbit's happy in a field of carrots
The simplest roost is good enough for parrots.
The snail, slowly crawling always leaves its trace
Why, then, do I always feel I'm lost in space?

The hippopotamus basks in the river mud
The cow, in its field, contentedly chews its cud
The shark makes its home in the deep blue sea
The eagle builds its nest in the tallest tree
The deer runs through the woods with utter grace
It seems each being has found its own space.

Posing the question I must now embrace,
Why have I never found my rightful place?

THANKSGIVING

I was born on this farm, lived here all of my life
With the farmer, his two kids and the farmer's wife.
They all love the fall and here are the reasons
Why they think it's the best of all seasons.

The farmer loves it for the fall crops he can sell,
His wife for the pumpkin pies she bakes so well,
Their son loves it because he also loves football,
And their daughter loves its bright foliage and all.

They all love the fall, also, because of Thanksgiving
Which they make each year a high point of their living.
They look forward to Thanksgiving Day and a great feast
With lots of food of which roast turkey's hardly the least.

Thanksgiving Day is coming soon and they're all happy and perky,
But not me—you see, I'm the poor Thanksgiving turkey.

A GARDEN OF MY OWN

I love to sit in public gardens filled with lovely flow'rs,
There to repose and relax amid the beauty for hours and hours.
To view the many-hued flow'rs that are blooming there,
And to savor their bouquet which richly fills the air.
'Tis then I think I'd like to have a garden of my own some day,
Where I could visit the flow'rs and, even spend all day.
But then I think you don't plant flow'rs and just watch them grow,
You have to till the soil, rake it and also sometimes hoe.
Decide what flow'rs you want to plant and go buy the seeds,
You must fertilize the soil, water it, and constantly pull weeds.
And then when those seeds become strong and healthy plants,
They are attacked and killed by aphids, spiders, mites and ants.

TWO STRANGE OLD BIRDS

A strange old bird is the ostrich
When things start to get out of hand,
He just sticks his head in the sand
Which I think is quite perpostrich.

A strange old bird's this flamingo
He'll stand on one leg, all day in the drink,
Which can lead one only to think
He must be a little bit dingo.

SNOWFALL

From the dark and wintry sky beclouded
'Til the earth in vestal white's enshrouded
Fall crystal flakes from God's own magic brush
To paint our world in pristine beauty lush
And though I always love to see it snow
I always dread it, too, because I know
That what today may seem so rich and plush
Will tomorrow be but brown and ugly slush.

MARCH INTO SPRING

Please think not of March as the Devil's own pox
Dwell not on its blustery winds or cold wint'ry snow
Think kindly of March as you await the spring equinox
Welcome the jonquils that will rise from below!

Yes, March comes in like a lion, but goes out like a lamb,
For it's all part of heaven's well-ordered plan.
So think not of March as any negative thing,
Just remember, it's March that brings us to spring.

The Arts

THE OPERA FROM HELL
An analytical, critical and poetical look at
Orfeo and Euridice, *an Opera by Gluck.*

I went to the Opera House to have a good look
At Orfeo and Euridice, an opera by Gluck
I hesitated, at first, but then said, Oh well!
No Opera can be but so bad if it takes place in hell.

I thought with some real great, incredible luck
This opera might be more than opera's usual muck
Well, lo and behold, in one of opera's great surprises
The soprano's dead before the curtain even rises.

Sad Orfeo is mourning his wife Euridice's fate
And pleading with the Gods that it not be too late
For her to come back, and though it may really sound stupid
He is soon joined by the God of Love, some guy named Cupid

Cupid tells him because of his devotion and fervent love
He can descend into Hades and return her above.
There's one condition that he must meet, without any slack,
He can't look at Euridice while he's bringing her back.

Orfeo leaves and is soon at Hell's reception center
Where he's halted by the Furies who won't let him enter.
But Orfeo again pleads his love for his wife so true
That the Furies quickly relent and let him pass through.

Soon Euridice's on her way home, Orfeo by her side
But, like all women, Euridice wasn't satisfied.
He wouldn't look at her, she whined, he wasn't committed
And Orfeo, being a mere man, just meekly submitted.
So he fastened on Euridice his love-jaundiced eye

And damned if she didn't for the second time, just up and die
As last, the soprano is dead as we all had expected
But not for long for, once again, she gets resurrected.

For Cupid, impressed by Orfeo's deep love for his wife
Decides to resurrect her again and give her new life,
The lovers are happily rejoined with no further pall
Confirming Cupid's motto, which is you know, "Love Conquers All!"

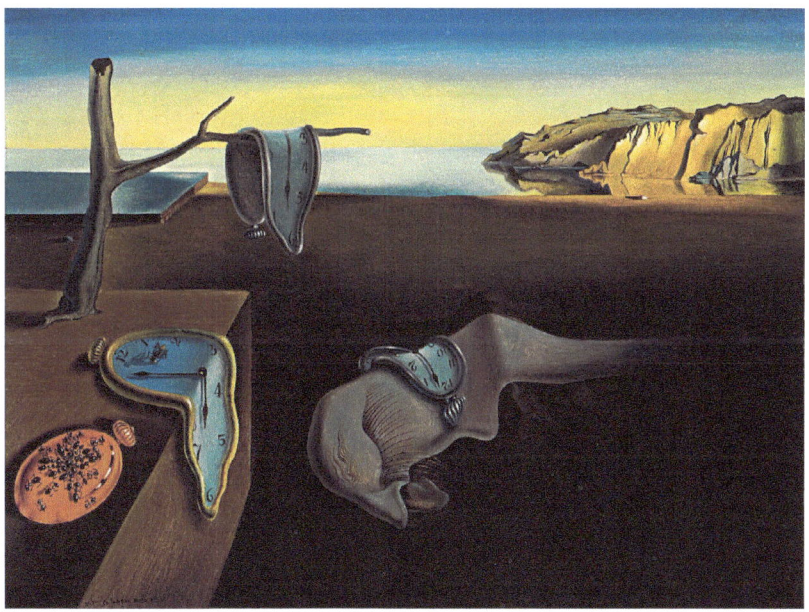

OH HELL! DALI!
Inspired by Salvador Dali's The Persistence of Memory, *1931*

The watch is sliding right off the table?
The artist who drew it surely can't be stable.
And the woman's boobs are on her back, you see!
Doesn't the artist know where a woman's boobs should be?
Some folks call this stuff art, but I call it folly.
I guess I'm not persuaded by the works of Salvador Dali.

I'M OUTTA HERE
Inspired by Gustave Dore's The Neophyte, *1868*

What, in God's name, am I doing here?
    My dreams have led me here!
My dreams, my dreams! Which only yesterday
    Were upward winging like a lark
    From the meadow rising.
My dreams, my dreams! Which today are falling,
    Falling like a stone which has broken
    Loose from the mountain top.
My dreams, my dreams! Have they failed me,
    Led me to this impossible place
    Where my youth is to be devoured
    By these dragons of senility, futility,
    Boredom and lonesomeness?
My dreams, my dreams! Do I still have any dreams left?
My dreams, my dreams! Yes, I do still have dreams.
    For now my dreams are of escaping this plight.
    So it's over the wall and outta here I go tonight!

THE MASTICATION, REGURGITATION AND ENCAPSULATION OF SHAKESPEARE'S ROMEO AND JULIET

In ancient Verona, a commune in Italy,
Like our own West Virginia's Hatfield's and McCoys.
The Capulets and Montagues feuded bitterly
So Capulet girls couldn't date Montague boys.
But Juliet Capulet and Romeo Montague
They fell madly in love and sought to wed each other
But doing so wasn't easy, believe me, it's true
For it didn't please Juliet's father and mother
Who urged her to wed a noble lad, Paris,
Whose sincerest affections by Juliet were spurned
For a girl must experience true love when she marries
So her fond affections toward Romeo she turned.
Well, this story turns out to be a real thriller
But most of what happens is really just filler.
For the bottom line's this: Two who would love, instead
By their own hands, because of love, wind up dead.

In this very play Shakespeare himself said, "Love is Blind"
For who knows who will get stung by an arrow from Cupid
But after having read this play, I really do find
That love's not only blind, but it's also stupid.

But it's often been said and I believe it is true
That from all tragedy some good must also ensue.
So both Capulets and Montagues, filled with much grief,
Decided to shake hands and they turned over a new leaf.
Thus, while Romeo and Juliet both lost their lives,
'Tis said, between their families, harmony now thrives.

ROSES IN BLOOM

A poem in tanka form Inspired by Pierre-Auguste Renoir's The Daughters of Durand-Ruel, *1882*

Two beautiful girls
Pose in a garden bower,
Like roses in bloom,
Captured by the artist's brush
That they might bloom forever.

COLORS
Inspired by Arshile Gorky's Still Life, *1929*

Colors! Red, yellow, blue, black, brown, white,
    hurtling toward you like shrapnel from an
    exploding artillery shell.

Colors! Which neither mix nor blend, ever in
    contrast, opposing and clashing
    with one another.

Colors! One can sense the vibrations emanating
    from this explosion of colors.

ANTIGONE IN A NUTSHELL

It really gave me a big, bad case of the old Heebie-Jeebs,
Sophocles' terrible, tragic story of Greece's ancient Thebes.
And of its unbelievably cruel king, who was named Creon
Whose cold, cold heart, it was said, pumped not only human blood, but pure Freon.
Well, this tragic story is firmly founded on this sad thesis.
Two brothers by the names of Eteocles and Polyneices,
Fighting in a ware over Thebes, one defending, one attacking,
Fell in battle and were, both of them, to the Greek gods sent packing.
Eteocles was granted burial, but by Creon's edict
Polyneices lay exposed, by birds and dogs his bones to be picked.
When Creon's edict by the brothers' sister, Antigone, was heard
She took it upon herself to see that Polyneices' remains be interred.
Antigone was captured and brought before Creon for sentence
Which Creon decreed to be death since she showed no repentance.
Creon's son, Haemon, pleaded grace for her, to whom he was engaged
But cruel Creon refused and Haemon left, at Creon enraged.
Then Antigone was dispatched forthwith to face her certain doom
For Creon ordered, though alive she be sealed in a cave, her tomb.
Then, Creon fearing the Gods' vengeance, decided to grant her grace
And set out with his entourage to free her from that awful place.

Before he arrived he heard what sounded like Haemon's mad screaming
And sent his servants to see if 'twas Haemon or Creon's dreaming.
The servants found Antigone by a halter, quite dead, hanging,
While Haemon against the tomb's wall, his head, in anguish was banging.
Creon, to offer Haemon consolation, rushed quickly forward
But, alas, Haemon, seeking death, threw himself upon his own sword.
Then, while Creon bore home his son's corpse, a messenger went ahead
To announce Haemon's fate and, thus, Eurydice learned her son's death.
Then Eurydice, the wife of Creon, to her house did stagger
Where she took her own life at the point of a very sharp dagger.
Finally, Creon arrived at Thebes bearing Haemon on his bier
Where, "Eurydice is dead, too" were the first words to reach his ear.
Creon, now, would change the cruel path he had chosen, but 'twas too late.
So heed this, "be sure of what you're doing, 'fore you play with fate."
Well, I've said quite enough about this tragic play, for goodness' sake
Except to say, with all those deaths, what a great op'ra it would make.

WHO HAS THE LAST LAUGH NOW!
Inspired by Roy Lichtenstein's Live Ammo, 1962

High up in a cloudless, yet dangerous sky
For you and me, twas a case of do or die
For we were engaged in a deadly dog fight
You were on my tail and I was filled with fright
I could sense your evil laugh as you prepared to fire,
But I pulled back on my stick and zoomed much high'r
Then I made a sudden and wide, looping turn
And, lo and behold, I was at your stern.
I laughed as my live ammo struck your plane—KA-POW!
So it's Ha! Ha! Ha! Who has the last laugh now?

THE JAZZ SINGER
Inspired by Franz Kline's Hot Jazz, *1940*

Hot Jazz! Pulsing, throbbing, surging,
      filling one's emotions.
Like colors, changing in tone and intensity
      from the soft, pastel moan of the saxophone
      to the bright, golden blare of the trumpet.
Its tempo set by the light, sparkling rhythm of the piano
      and the dull thump, thump, thump of the drum,
Contrasting, yet in tune with the natural wood tones
      of the piano and the dark jackets of the musicians.
In the center of it all stands the Jazz Singer,
      dominating the musicians as the blue of her gown
      dominates the painting.
I can hear her throaty voice, above the music,
      belting out her song of unrequited love.

FEELINGS?
Inspired by Paul Stephenson's The Wounded Indian, *1850*

What are you feeling now, wounded warrior?
Pain?
>Pain from the arrow which has wounded you?
>Pain from the agony of defeat?

Fear?
>Fear of joining your ancestors, lest they look
>Upon you with scorn for having been defeated in battle?

Anticipation?
>Anticipation that your ancestors will honor you as
>A brave warrior who fought valiantly for his tribe
>Before he was felled by that arrow?

Hatred?
>Hatred for the one whose arrow brought you down?

Respect?
>Respect for the brave warrior who so grievously wounded you
>While fighting valiantly for his tribe?

Sorrow?
>But wait-I forget! You have no feelings
>For you are but a slab of cold mountain stone
>Fashioned by a crafty artisan to arouse emotions
>In sentimental souls such as I.

THEY'RE ALL ALIKE

I wrote this poem about Mozart's Cosi Fan Tutti
Not just because of its wonderful, musical beauty
But because I also considered it my poetic duty.
To a poet its character's names are really a pill.
First there's Guglielmo who for brevity we'll call Bill
And Farendo, his good friend and Don Alfonso, their pal.
Who for purposes of rhyming we're going to call Al.
Next, there's Fioroiligi, Bill's girl, whom you can call what you please
For pronouncing her name could easily buckle one's knees.
And her sister who goes by the name of Dorabella
Who claims Farendo as her very own special fella.
Finally, there is one more character, named Despina
Who is the sisters' own personal maid and house cleaner
Now the scene is set for me to tell you the whole damned plot
But I do not want to spoil it for you, so I will not.
Except to tell you of the opera's principle theme
When Al and Despina join in a scheme
To get Bill and Farendo to test their girls' virtue.
An exercise they should have known can only hurt you
Well, I like this opera a lot, but I have one complaint.
The sopranos don't die, though they occasionally faint
And the opera ends happily without solving man's plight
That, no man can trust a woman when she's out of his sight.

THE CURTAIN DESCENDS

The role's been fully played, the show has run,
A good performance, with few prizes won.
There are no encores and no curtain calls,
No applause resonating off the walls.
And, though the show, by many, was enjoyed,
The house lights are dark and the stage now void.
Forgotten are the spotlights; forgotten, the clever sets,
How soon? How soon? Too soon, the audience forgets.

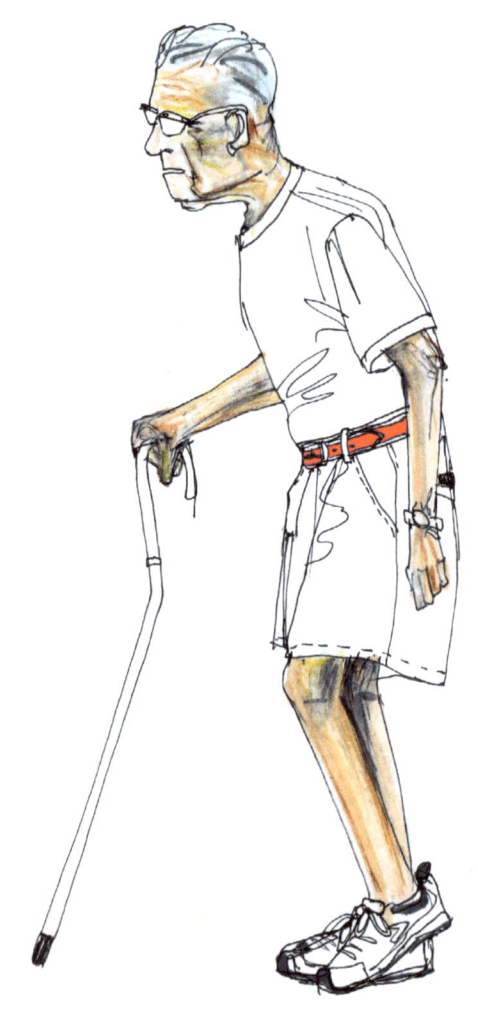

Age, Health & Lifestyle

THE PHYSICAL EXAM
Dedicated to Robert F. Mann, M.D., March 2007

I went to my doctor for a physical exam
To find out how healthy I really am.
He said, "Come in and get completely undressed."
Then he scanned my stomach and x-rayed my chest,
He listened to my heart with his stethoscope,
No irregularities, exactly my hope.
He tested my blood and, also, my urine
And the test results were quite reassuring.
He looked into my ears and deep into my eyes
And while depressing my tongue made me say AHS
He checked me to see if I had a hernia,
But how he did it really shouldn't concern ya.
He even looked up both sides of my nose,
Then counted my fingers and, also, my toes.
Then, I said, "Well, that's the end of that, I guess,"
But he said, "No, there's one more test before you can dress."
Then, while placing a rubber glove on his hand
He said, "Bend over now right where you stand."
And then I knew what was really at stake,
And I cried, "No! No! Please no, for goodness sake!"
But the doctor wasn't playing some practical joke.
He was going to give me that old proctologist poke.

TEN DAYS OUT OF MY GOLDEN YEARS

On day one I was examined by my G.P.
And 350 dollars was the doctor's fee.

The second day my heart doctor said, "Your heart's out of rhythm,"
And for these words 400 dollars I had to give 'im.

The third day my urologist said, "Your prostate's enlarged,"
And 350 dollars is the amount he charged.

The fourth day my gastroenterologist said, "You have reflux,"
And this diagnosis cost me over 300 bucks.

The fifth day my ophthalmologist said I had macular
And I won't say what he charged but it was spectacular.

The sixth day my podiatrist removed a callous.
Judging from his fee, this guy must live in a palace.

The seventh day my audiologist, whose name is Jeff,
Got 200 dollars for telling me I was deaf.

The eighth day my chiropractor cracked my neck,
And said 300 dollars, please, cash, credit card or check.

The ninth day, Saturday, I had the E.R. order me a pill,
I don't know what they charged. They're still padding the bill.

The tenth day, Sunday, my preacher said, "Your life's full of sin,
So throw all your money in the collection bin."

Despite what they all charged, my ailments haven't
  depreciated,
But the pills they prescribed my pharmacist sure appreciated.

A WELL-BALANCED DIET

People always try to define a "well-balanced" diet.
The numbers are few who, at least once, didn't try it.
The U.S.D.A. defined it in the form of a pyramid,
Which was later found to be not quite valid.
Once there was a diet people called grapefruit

And I've read of Aborigines who ate nothing but root,
The vegetarians, you know, will never eat any meat,
While others think a hot dog's a great thing to eat.
Today's rage is the diet of the venerable Dr. Atkins
Which, if followed, will make us all thin as hat pins.
There's the low fat, no fat, low carb, no carb and South Beach.
Diets which people follow and about which many will preach,
Frankly, all this confusion about diet I'd really like to smother,
'Cause my best diet is a beer in one hand, pretzel, the other.

TROPHIES

When young, I wasn't very good at sports
Baseball, football, track or any other sorts
And each time a race had been fully run
Twas some other guy who had the trophy won.

But people said "keep trying, you'll have your trophies too"
Now what those people said has at last come true.
For I've grown old and have my own trophies now, you see.
But, alas, they're called "a-trophy" and "dys-trophy".

HOUSE FOR SALE

There's a sign in my front yard – House for Sale
If this old house could talk, OH! What a tale
Of love and hope and happiness I would spin
About the lives of those who have lived within
My sheltering, protective room and wall;
Of children's toy and game or soccer ball,
Of Easter egg, Thanksgiving feast and other fun,
Of neighbor kid who often up my stairs did run,
Of little boy who played with soldiers on my floor,
Of Christmas wreath you've hung on my front door,

Of candle burned on birthday cake and at Christmas time,
Of baby's cry or dog that barked at doorbell chime
Which heralded neighbor, friend or sometimes stranger,
Of peaceful, quiet, protected times and also times of danger,
Of much happiness and, yes, some sadness, too.
Yet through it all I was surely good to you.
House for Sale? – I suppose I should from my rafters cry,
Oh! How could you sell me, how could you, why?
But I don't cry for I understand what you must do.
I know that time has changed us both, both me and you
And I know that I will stay within your heart,
For memories will make it so we'll never part.
House for Sale? When I am sold, I know I'll miss you
But if I could talk I know from my wall would issue
Tales of love and hope and happiness I'd spin
About the lives of those who are yet to live within
My sheltering, protective room and wall.
I've been sold? Goodbye! Good Luck! I love you all!

PARADOX

Was God with man's creation cheating
When he made our youth so very fleeting
Gave us so many things for which to yearn
And so many lessons that we'd want to learn
Yet when He gave us the wisdom to pursue 'em
At the same time made us too old and tired to do 'em?

HOPIN'

I was hopin'
To stop mopin'
'Stead of gropin'
To start copin'.

MEMORIES AND DREAMS

When we are young it most surely seems
Our life is filled which naught but dreams
Of things that add zest to our life's flavor
A parade of things we wish to taste and savor
But as we age our dreams begin to dim and fade
And only mem'ries, then, march in life's parade.
For mem'ries replace our dreams until, at last,
All our dreams by mem'ries are surpassed
But our dreams by mem'ries are not fully stilled
For aren't mem'ries just our dreams fulfilled.

WHEN I'M GONE

I worry not that I, too, must die
So, please, o'er my grave let no one cry
When I'm gone, do not grieve for me
Just let them take me out and bury me
Someplace that's wide and wild and free
And there I'll rest forever in perfect peace
'Til all human mem'ries of me shall cease
One thought of death, though, leaves me forlorn.
Who will wind my wrist watch when I'm gone?

LIFE'S SHORT—SO EAT DESSERT FIRST

Celebrate your life as though singing a glorious song,
Dance, with joy every step of your life's journey,
Just remember, it won't be too terribly long
Before they roll you outta here on a gurney.

THAT'S FOR CERTAIN

My old, old body is a-aching and a-hurting
For years, with that old grim reaper, I've been a-flirting.
And I know there ain't but two things that's a-certain,
That's the gov'nment's taxes and that old dark, black curtain.

A SHOPPER'S LAMENT
Dedicated to Sally Clay

It's morning, I'm awake, but still in my bed
I shouldn't be lying around like an old sleepy head
I should be rushing out my door, with a joyous shout
While from my pockets pulling my credit cards out
And gathering all the money I can beg, steal and borrow
'Cause there's only one shopping day left 'til tomorrow.

THE ROAD MORE TRAVEL'D

I now travel on a narrow, rutted road
While bearing a far, far too heavy load.
This road, so wide and smooth at its beginning,
Which, as I travel, keeps roughening and thinning.
For a long time on this road I've been traveling,
A once pleasant journey that's now unraveling.
Despite the long, long time on this road I've spent,
I never knew just where it really went.
Until a certain point of no return I'd crossed
To realize my once precious youth had now been lost.
And since my precious youth I cannot save,
Can it be this road now leads only to the grave?

SECRET GARDENS

I sit alone but I'm not lonely
Viewing blossoms that bloom only
In the secret gardens of my mind.

Some blossoms warm with hope and love
Brighter than summer stars above
In the secret gardens of my mind.

Some blossoms wilted, brown and faded
Flowers of a past that now seems jaded
In the secret gardens of my mind.

Some are strangling vines that snarl all
That tried to grow within the wall
In the secret gardens of my mind.

From what seed do they derive
Are they real? Are they alive?
In the secret gardens of my mind.
Some are memories, some are dreams
But none is ever what it really seems
In the secret gardens of my mind.

MORNING

You know at the sun-light's first dawning,
That it is, once again, early morning.
And, oh, how I hate to get up so early,
'Cause it makes me feel grumpy and surly.
Though, I have nothing against morning, I guess.
I should stand up and readily confess,
That I'd be singing a much happier tune
If morning started just a tad later . . . say Noon?

TEMPTATION VERSE

Temptation wingeth as the lark
Satan prospers in the dark
So heed my message, though it's stark,
Don't go petting in the park!

SHORT CIRCUITS

If our brains have one hundred billion neutron
And ten to the fourteenth power of synapses.
Why, then, must we all have to always endure on,
So dog-goned many memory lapses?

BALLS

Baseball, football and tennis are all
Games which require the use of a ball.
Dominoes, poker and pitch-a-penny
Are all games that don't require any.
And, as for golf, this, my friends, is also true,
It takes a lot of balls to play golf the way I do.

WHEN TWO HEARTS COLLIDE

It's like the sun and earth together crashing,
Like a great tidal wave rolling and splashing.
Life all of God's birds beautifully singing,
Like all the world's church bells chiming and ringing.
Like having your heart filled with nothing but pride,
That's what it's like when two hearts collide.

And since you grow older and continue to mature,
The ardor may fade, but the love remains sure.
It's like the fruit ripening and sweetening on the tree,
It's like I've become you and you've become me.
It's like having heaven's portals opened wide.
That's what it's like when two hearts collide.

You may grow even older and your steps may falter,
But it's like that day you knelt at the altar,
For tho age may now make you appear bent and wrinkled,
It's like your hearts, with love, were forever sprinkled.
Because you still walk together, hand in hand, side by side,
That's what it's like when two hearts collide.

ETERNITY

Endless time, which itself, reaches from infinity to infinity,
Offers only a small measure of itself for both you and me.
For, like a speck of sulfur, which ignited, flares then quickly dies,
We, too, who pass our way beneath unmeasured skies.
Briefly glow then we, too, die. Each in our own turn,
'Tis from the unknown we flow and to the unknown that we return.

THERE IS NO ART IN FAILURE: AUTOBIOGRAPHY OF A LOSER

I know not how my life will end,
    I can't remember how it st_____ed.
But each path or life I've had to wend,
    With stores of opportunity was ch_____ed.
Yet each time, to pick one up, I dared to bend,
    I either split my pants . . . Or f_____ed.

LIFE IS JUST A BOWL OF CHERRIES

Life is just a bowl of cherries, it has been spoken.
Implying life's a chain of happiness that's never broken.
But we all know that's just not really true
For life's full of pain and sorrow, for both me and you
Yet, despite that, the analogy still aptly fits.
For the cherries in that bowl, we all know, have pits.

A LIFE OF BIBLICAL IMPORT

I once spent a lot of time in sad lament
Despite the many gifts I'd been given
O'er how my life had been really spent,
As though in a vacuum I had been livin'.
Whenever opportunity chanced to look my way
I just ignored it and continued in my rut.
No one would even give me the day
Or pay attention to, or heed me, but
Although I wasn't good at anything, even sport
And every time I was challenged always took a pass,
I now know my life is one of biblical import
For I'm older than Methuselah and dumb as Balaan's ass.

DEATH DANCES ROUND MY BED AT NIGHT

When at dark of night I wake, I'm sorely filled with fright,
For, then, death comes to dance around my bed at night.
So, if you can, please solve for me this intriguing riddle,
Does death so dance because Satan plays his fiddle,
Or does Satan play his fiddle because death so dances
With joy as my life toward it so rapidly advances?
Such dark of night brings fear and fills my heart with terror
For, then, death beckons me, darkly, as through a mirror

I pass those nights in stark reality and I have no dreams.
Yet from eternity I hear my own tortured screams,
But why should I fear death so deeply and so badly?
Why should I not face it openly and, yet, even gladly?
For death surely brings a peace that all persons crave,
And I know one's life ends not in a cold and lonely grave.

A LITTLE LOVE FROM YOU

When I'm feeling all lost and lonely
My thoughts turn toward you only
And all my troubles just go away
So please believe me when I say:
All I need's a little love from you.

I don't need no therapy session
To rid me of my depression
And lots of pills in great big doses
Won't cure me of my neuroses
All I need's a little love from you.

Whenever I feel all sad and blue
My thoughts always turn to you
And all my worldly cares just take a flight
So please believe what I say is right:
All I need's a little love from you.
I don't need no electric shock therapy
To make me act sweet and syrupy
Don't need no darned psychoanalyst
Or Dr. Ruth, talk show panelist
All I need's a little love from you.

All those times when I start feeling low
It's straight to you I want to go
For I know my feelings then will peak

So please believe these words I speak:
All I need's a little love from you.

I don't need no darned lobotomy
Or folks to think a lotta me
And you know those flowers I sent ya,
Won't cure me of my dementia.
All I need's a little love from you.

When I'm sad and life's no longer fun
It's straight to your warm arms I run
For there I know I will find your love,
So please know this, all else above:
All I need's a little love from you.

I don't need no doctor's ordered rest
To keep me from getting depressed
And I don't need no hypnotic spell
To make me feel secure and well
All I need's a little love from you.

HAIKU! GESUNDHEIT!

A mother dreads war
      As the lamb fears the lion
            Thus she often weeps.

The tree of true life
      Springs from the rich soil of faith
            And shall never die.

In a manger low
      With the oxen lay a child
            Peace, goodwill to all.

WRINKLES

I'm delighted to have lived to this ripe old age.
But the guy who coined the term "Golden Years" is no sage
For when I move, now my joints are all sore and creaky
And at inappropriate times my bladder's a tad leaky.
I'm afflicted with numerous aches and many sharp pains
And I even have a terrible case of varicose veins.
I now have arthritis, phlebitis and, also, sciatica
And in order to go I have to take Sal Hepatica.
My grandchildren come visit and say, "Pick me up, Gramps"
I bend to do so, but can't because I have cramps.
Well, that's how it is when you've lived past your prime,
You're glad to be alive, but you hurt all the time
But there's one blessing of old age, I often assert,
By saying, "Thank you, dear Lord, that wrinkles don't hurt."

Travel & Holidays

A WEE BIT OF ENGLAND

I. WORCESTER CATHEDRAL

As I stood beside Worcester's river Severn,
I felt as though my heart was touched by heaven.
Why, in this place, have you been so inspired,
My deeply doubting mind, at first, inquired?
But when Worcester Cathedral's reaching spires I spied,
I knew, for in this place, God is glorified.

II. GLOUCESTER CATHEDRAL

As I walked along Gloucester's Westgate Street,
I felt the angels' clouds beneath my feet.
Why, in this place, do you feel so high and free,
My deeply doubting mind inquired of me?
See the cathedral's spires rising toward the skies,
In this place, replied I, could one feel otherwise?

III. IN BATH

In Bath, they had an idea
    That really wasn't shoddy
They built themselves public baths
    For cleansing of the body.

Then they had a new idea
    That wasn't really shabby.
For cleansing of the souls,
    They built themselves and abbey.

Then they had a great idea
    That really wasn't funny.
They turned them into tourist traps
    And made a lot of money.

IV GOD SAVE THE QUEEN

When an English child for the first speaks,
You'll near these words between its shrieks.
    God save the Queen!

Before English youth's games can get underway,
These inspiring words they first must say
    God save the Queen!

When an English lad goes to pick up his date,
He must, for her father, three times must state.
    God save the Queen!

After the cathedral bell has been loudly rung,
At ev'ry evensong these words are sung.
    God save the Queen!

If an Englishman wants some fish and chips,
He must say before he can take his nips.
    God save the Queen!

And if he is an M.P., highly respected,
Here are the words that got him elected.
    God save the Queen!

When an Englishman has grown old and weak,
He'll still find strength, these words to speak.
    God save the Queen!

And when, at last, it's come his time to die,
Those same words will be his last good-bye.
    God save the Queen!

V.   GREEN AND PLEASANT LAND

As through the English countryside we rolled,
Past lush, green fields and gently swelling wold
I thought of life stories left heretofore untold
Stories that, perhaps, will never yet unfold
Of times when nightly, from the skies, bombs had thundered
And how often, then, in admiration I had wondered
How the British could go to bed, in fear, each night,
Yet rise, each morn, to bravely carry on the fight.
To save home, villages, church and rustic pub?
But as Shakespeare once said, "Ah, there's the rub."
For what sort of man is he, who would not stand
To save his home in this green and pleasant land?

OUTER BANKS

Each time I walk along that barren barrier beach
I feel a part of heaven has come within my reach.
Some days, the sea rolls gently in to wash upon the shore
Other days, white-capped crests break with thund'rous roar
Sea oats dance upon the dunes to a rhythmic ocean breeze.
While I walk along the shore, the ocean swirling at my knees
I see porpoises play and frolic out on the open sea
Much like a frisky colt might gambol on the lea
I love to watch the shore birds, sea gulls, pipers, terns,
As each, from the sea and sand, its own livelihood it earns.
And there's little more enchanting for which I, perhaps, might wish
Than the graceful flight of pelicans as they search the sea for fish.
Yes, the shore and the ocean, whether wild or still and calm,
For my troubled inner self provide the perfect balm
So, when I made my list of things for which to give God thanks
High on that list I placed North Carolina's Outer Banks.

SAN FRANCISCO

Ol' John Sutter, in a stream near his mill
Found some gold with which his pockets he'd fill
He tried to keep it quiet but the secret got out,
"There's gold in California, it's just lying about."
From near and far, then, the 49ers all came,
Each seeking to find his own fortune and fame.
They staked out, they claimed. They dug and they mined,
Each an enormous nugget he prayed he would find
But it wasn't to be, it just didn't pan out
And soon, for most, all their resources ran out.
So without the fortune for which they had prayed,
They all found jobs and in the area they stayed
And that's how Yerba Buena, a small trading post
Became San Francisco, that great city now loved by most.

THE BAH! HUMBUG! TREE

Have you heard the story of the Bah! Humbug! Tree?
It blooms each December both for you and for me.
It's not very pretty, I'm sure you'll agree,
But you'll come to love it, just you wait and see.
It's fruit isn't sweet and it's the color of rouge,
And it was first planted and grown by a fellow named Scrooge,
So learning to love it will take an effort that's huge,
But once that you do you'll not seek refuge
In Christmases past or any Christmas to be
For your life will be as bright as a real Christmas tree.
Your memory of Scrooge may be just a Bah! Humbug! Or three
But later in life he was filled with Christmas spirit, you see
Which he got from eating the fruit of his Bah! Humbug! Tree.
So if your life's not filled with Christmas spirit, but you want it to be,
You don't need Christmases past or any Christmas to be
All you need is to eat the fruit of your own Bah! Humbug! Tree.

HAVE YOURSELF A FURRY LITTLE CHRISTMAS
Dedicated to Sally, "Nutmeg" and "Honey"

When I was just a little child, not even ten, as yet
All I wanted for my Christmas was my very own pet.
Of course, I felt I should let my mother and father know,
But they responded, both loud and clear, "No, no, no, no, no!"
When I asked them "why not" they had replied, "Well, just because."
And that's when I took my Christmas wish right to Santa Claus
So it was late Christmas Eve night or early Christmas morn,
When by anticipation from my warm bed I was torn
To see if Santa Claus had already been at our house
And I crept down the stairs, quiet as a non-stirring mouse.
Then I saw our tree lit up, aglow like never before
With lots of packages under it, all over the floor
One package in particular, looked unusual to me
Just an old cardboard box, what in the world could it be?
I slowly approached the tree, with no sounds, even verbals
And when I opened that box, inside were two cute, little gerbils
Then Santa Claus' sleigh bells, on our roof top, jingled and rang,
While "Have yourself a furry little Christmas," Santa Claus sang.

SANTA'S RETIREMENT

'Twas a few years ago on December twenty-third
The following lament from the North Pole was heard.

For centuries now I've driven this old sled
Pulled by reindeer, one with nose cherry red
At every house I'm expected on Christmas Eve night
Making a schedule that's always too tight
At each house, on cookies and milk, I'm expected to snack
Until my stomach's as big as the sack on my back
And the gifts the children requested in terms quite out-spoken
On the day after Christmas lie shattered and broken

But the children don't care. You need have nary a fear
For, by then, they're requesting their gifts for Christmas next year
So for this lousy job I've lost all my desire.
And tomorrow morning early, I'm going to retire.

Now, you listen to me, Santa, said Mrs. Santa Claus
Before you retire, take a moment, give pause
What would you do, you don't even play golf
And you know how much you'd miss Rudolph
Yes, it's true your schedule's really quite hectic.
But you'll disappoint millions if you don't show when expected.
And you don't have to get fat, between Christmases you could go on a diet
I've told you this before, but you never would try it.
And some children, their gifts, they do break up or shatter
But at Christmas isn't it the children themselves who really do matter
Even those children who break up their gifts all love you, dear
And you're always the first to ask what they want for Christmas next year.

So you should change your plans to give up employment
Or come Christmas Eve night, you'll have no enjoyment.

You know, Mrs. Claus, said Santa, I believe you are right
Now I'm looking forward to Christmas Eve night
So tell Donder and Blitzen and all the other reindeer,
We'll make our Christmas Eve rounds as usual this year.

A LETTER FROM SANTA

In a break from a tradition quite old
And with pen strokes exceptionally bold
Santa set the whole world right back on its ear
By telling kids what he wants for Christmas this year.

And since I couldn't have said it, myself, any better
I'll just read to you Santa's whole doggone letter:

Dear Kids: I know you're supposed to write me
A nice letter each year to invite me
To come to your house with goodies and toys
For all of you who've been good girls and boys.
But this year I'm writing you instead, you see,
To tell you what you can do this year for me.
Now, please don't worry, I'll not disappoint ya,
With goodies and toys, I still plan to anoint ya.
But those cookies and milk you leave me as a snack
I really wish that you'd hold them all back.
Cookies and milk are ok for my elves and reindeer
But as for old Santa himself, I'd rather have pretzels and beer.

A SMOKY CHRISTMAS

It was early Christmas morning when I suddenly awoke
Something was badly wrong, the house was filled with smoke.
It was really scary, the situation was truly dire,
With all that smoke, we thought, the house must be on fire.
To determine what was wrong we all decided to pitch in
We checked out the bathroom and then moved on to the kitchen.
We searched the bedrooms, the halls, the pantry and the den,
We checked out our old house from its beginning to its end.
But there was no trace of fire, at least, that we could see
So we moved to the living room to check the lights that were on
 our tree.
If our house is on fire, we thought, this Christmas won't be any fun
So we started panicking and had decided to dial 911
When I saw the fireplace where smoldering embers were dying
And, lo and behold, out of that fireplace the smoke was fairly flying
Then suddenly I realized what was wrong, Yes I did, by Jiminy!
Jolly old Santa Claus had gotten stuck in our chimney.

I'M CANCELING CHRISTMAS THIS YEAR

I told you kids you better be good
And do all the things you knew you should
But, oh now, you just had to be bad.
So, now, you'll hear this from your dear old Dad.
I'm canceling Christmas this year!

I'm canceling Christmas this year.
No holly, no eggnog, no cheer
No carols to hum,
And Santa won't come.
I'm canceling Christmas this year!

I'm canceling Christmas this year,
There'll be no mistletoe here.
This may sound fanatic,
But our tree will stay in the attic.
I'm canceling Christmas this year!

I'm canceling Christmas this year,
And Christmas Eve, also, I fear.
There'll be no wreath on our door,
And your gifts will stay in the store.
I'm canceling Christmas this year!

I'm canceling Christmas this year,
Though it pains me as it draws near.
We won't have a turkey,
We'll all dine on beef jerky.
I'm canceling Christmas this year!

I'm canceling Christmas this year,
Though I'm shedding many a tear.
There'll be no nuts and no candy,
And no cookies so handy,
I'm canceling Christmas this year!

I'm canceling Christmas this year,
I assure you, in this, I'm sincere.
There'll be no fun, and no frolic
There'll be nothing but colic.
I'm canceling Christmas this year!

I'm canceling Christmas this year,
As mean as this to you may appear.
There'll be no yuletide good wishes,
Or special holiday dishes.
I'm canceling Christmas this year!

I'm canceling Christmas this year,
There'll be no joy around here,
No bright star will be shining,
Of Christmases past you'll be pining.
I'm canceling Christmas this year!

I'm canceling Christmas this year,
The season will be dingy and drear.
You kids may hang up your socks,
But I'm gonna fill them with rocks.
I'm canceling Christmas this year!

I'm canceling Christmas this year.
The reason must be perfectly clear.
You kids knew how to behave,
If Christmas you'd wanted to save.
I'm canceling Christmas this year!

If what you've just heard makes you sad.
Wait! It's not really that bad,
Things are not what they seem,
It was all a bad dream
You kids were really quite good
And did most of the things that you should.
So we'll celebrate Christmas this year!

We'll celebrate Christmas this year!
There'll be holly and eggnog and cheer.
There'll be carols to hum
And Santa will come.
We'll celebrate Christmas this year!

    Merry Christmas

HALLOWEEN

Hobgoblins, vampires and yowling' black cats,
Sinister witches mixing potions in char-blackened vats,
Werewolf, ghost and other weird specter
Invading your space from hell's darkest sector
With groan, shriek, moan and other strange shout.
Is that what HALLOWEEN is really about?

Headless monster swinging the executioner's axe,
Messages from Satan received on your Fax,
Poltergeist, ghost and other vaporous spirit
Singing a dirge-Hark! Can't you hear it?
Is that what HALLOWEEN is really about?

Grave diggers and skeletons, made of nothing but bone,
The devil calling you up on your unlisted phone,
Spiders and lizards and poisonous snakes
Eating your pets like vanilla milk shakes,
And hissing, you're next, if you don't watch out.
Is that what HALLOWEEN is really about?

But wait! That sounds like wee, running feet,
And a strange cry at my door,
"Trick or Treat, Trick or Treat."
That one's a squirrel and the other a rabbit,
Hey, look over there, a nun in her habit,

And "Trick or Treat, Trick or Treat" is what they all shout.
Is that what HALLOWEEN is really about?

There's Batman and Robin, Roy Rogers and Trigger,
And Jack, of the bean stalk and the Giant who's bigger,
Little Orphan Annie and that must be Dale Evans,
Plus a dozen or so angels, come down from the Heavens,
And "Trick or Treat, Trick or Treat" is what they all shout
Is that what HALLOWEEN is really about?

There goes a scare-crow and an Indian brave,
And there's a prehistoric man just out of his cave,
Why, that one looks like ex-president Reagan,
And that must be Darth Vader pointing that ray gun,
And "Trick or Treat, Trick or Treat" is what they all shout
Is that what HALLOWEEN is really about?

Hobgoblins, ghosts, witches and tales of the grave,
Spiders and lizards, the Devil and all sorts of knave,
Or children in costume on wee, running feet,
Shouting at neighbors, "Trick or Treat, Trick or Treat"
That is what each of us, for ourselves, must find out.
Is that what HALLOWEEN is really about?

RESOLUTIONS

On January first, my resolutions
    Had all been spoken.
On January second, those resolutions
    Had all been broken.

HEARTBREAK

Love & Loss

CUPID'S GENTLE WOUND

When Cupid shoots his arrow in the air
It can find its target anywhere
And when I was young, oh! How I pined
That his arrow would someday find
Its target in the center of my heart
And its gentle wound therein impart
Feelings of love that would never end
And make a certain girl much more than friend.

But, alas, older now and wiser, too, I am
And I fear Cupid's dart game's just a sham.
So this warning to you, now, I must impart,
Beware, should Cupid's arrow strike your heart.
For I have learned as the years so quickly pass
That Cupid's gentle wound is just a big pain in the ass.

THREE DARK NIGHTS

Oh, I've known that dark night of the senses
When I've felt there was no one to love me
And that all others held themselves above me
Tho' I receive only what my own heart dispenses.
Oh, I've known that dark night of the spirit
When I've felt God does not hear my fervent plea
Yet how often does He lift his voice to me
And I'm too consumed with self to hear it?
Oh, I've known that dark night of the soul
When I've felt alone and God seemed, to me, not real
Yet I know the light I seek will never shine until
To God, I surrender my life's complete control.

A FEW LINES WRITTEN ON ONE OF MY BETTER DAYS

Tomorrow
All my laughter's drowned in tears,
All my courage dissolved in fears,
All my happiness ends in sorrow
Dear God, how I dread tomorrow!

Despair
Despair, deep down, dark and drear,
My heart's now empty of all but fear.
Oh, I hear that dreaded trumpeteer,
My heart's now empty of all but fear.
Funeral songs assail my ear,
My heart's now empty of all but fear.
Failing, falling, life grows mere,
My heart's now empty of all but fear.
The darkest angel's drawing near,
My heart's now empty of all but fear.
Coming, coming, coming! Here!
My heart's now empty of even fear.

The Past and the Future
There's been no rain, and the garden tree is dying.
I've shed no tears and yet, my heart is plainly crying.
I've seen no smile yet hear derisive laughter,
I find no joy in what has been and fear what may come after.

THE LANDFILL OF YESTERDAYS

Oh! How the months and years of life fly by so fast,
Rapidly transporting our future into the past.
Today's precious moments, filled with intrigue and mystery,
Will tomorrow be but a static part of history,

And whether one's life is drear or truly sublime,
We're all, helplessly, wafted on the wings of time,
For each precious moment of life will, too, be lost,
As, by time, on the landfill of yesterdays it's tossed.

IN APRIL

A gentle breath of fragrant April breeze
Whispers softly through the newly-budding trees.
Bright, yellow jonquils have risen from below
To replace the winter's cold and icy snow.
Other flowers, too, have raised their heads
As April's gentle showers washed their beds.
A robin comes to nest in a nearby tree
And sings for all its merry song of April glee.
Pearly beads of dew set the morning grass a-shimmering,
A restful respite afore summer's torrid simmering.
It seems God's in his heaven and all's right with the world,
When Spring's wond'rous beauty, in April, is unfurled.
But man from God's beauty is often torn asunder
As, in April, by the I.R.S's greedy plunder.

CHASTITY

If a woman is chased
She'll likely become unchaste
And
If a woman is unchased
She'll likely remain chaste
And if a woman is unchaste
She'll likely be chased
And
If a woman is chaste
She'll likely be unchased

A LOVELY FLOW'R
For Witt

Oh, lovely flow'r that ne'er fully bloom'd
Whose life to dark depression was so early doom'd
Once you were a seed of great promise to be sown
In life's garden where lovely flow'rs past had grown.

When planted, you soon became a tender sprig,
Upward reaching, so bravely striving to grow big
Soon a sturdy plant you were, with bright green leaves
Clinging to life like a baby to its mother cleaves.
Then into a healthy, flow'ring plant you'd grown
Enhancing the promise you'd til then shown.
Your petals, barely showing, were as bright as flame
And I was sure you'd be a flow'r of great acclaim.

But you never opened up your sepals wide
And kept those petals hidden deep, down inside.
For some dark reason, I ken not, and will never know,
Your flow'ring blossoms you could never fully show.

Though too little of your beauty could you ever let us see,
You always were a lovely flow'r, you see, to me.
For a precious gift from God you were, and still art
And your rare beauty is forever pressed within my heart.

LOVE IS A GAME

Love is a game that's played by fools.
A game that's played without any rules.
A game you might win; a game you might lose,
It all depends on the playmate you choose.

I'LL TELL YOU WHAT I'LL DO

If I had a flower garden,
I'll tell you what I'd do
I'd pick those lovely flowers
And give them all to you.

If I owned a great big yacht,
I'll tell you what I'd do
I'd put that yacht to sea
And you'd be my only crew.

If I had a million dollars
I'll tell you what I'd do.
I'd take that million dollars
And spend it all on you.

If I had a golden bracelet,
I'll tell you what I'd do.
I'd take it to the jeweler
And make sure it fit only you.

If I had a diamond ring,
I'll tell you what I'd do.
I'd put it on your finger
And spend all my life with you.

But I only have a kiss to give,
So I'll tell you what I'll do.
I'll place my lips on yours,
And whisper, I love you.

THE GRASS IS ALWAYS GREENEST

There once was a man in great discontent
Over how he felt his life was being spent.
He felt that his life was much too dark and drear,
That it would never change was his greatest fear.
One day he wandered down by the river wide,
And cast his eyes on the river's other side.
Where he saw a land with grass so rich and green,
It seemed the greenest grass he had ever seen.
And he thought, If I could reach that other side,
I'd live my life with both hope and joyful pride.
So he built himself a sturdy, wooden float
And, with it he crossed that separating moat.
At last, he thought, I'll find my fortune and fame
But he took one last look at "from whence he came,"
He looked back and to his dismay and surprise,
The grass there was now the greenest to his eyes.

OUR LOVE

Our love is like a song my heart's ever singing,
Like a bright silver bell that never stops ringing,
Or a welcoming beacon that's constantly shining
Ending my loneliness, yearning and pining.

Our love is like the flight of a bird, upwardly winging,
Like a rock of salvation to which I am clinging
Like possessing all of the world's treasure
Bringing me happiness beyond any measure.

Our love is like a beautiful stream, ever flowing
Like a star in the sky, forever twinkling and glowing.
Without our love my life would be bitter and stinging
So I know our love is a song my heart will never stop singing.

ON ADDICTION

Before taking up the habit, give this full attention,
Withdrawal's a lot more difficult than is abstention.

LIVIN' & LOVIN'

I've often been told that life is for livin'
And also that livin's for lovin'
Why, then, instead of our love givin'
Are we always pushin' and shovin'.

FAMILY LIFE

Family life, family life.
Tension and strife,
That's family life.

IN THE MATTER OF THE LORD VS. THE DEVIL

The Lord wanted to prosecute the devil,
But found the playing field wasn't level.
For where could the Lord find a lawyer
To prosecute Ebekinezer in hell?
In heaven he might find a sawyer
Or the farmer who lived in the dell.
There may be doctors in large numbers.
Some geniuses and many much dumber,
To mend the robes of the angels, a tailor
Or, in a sea of clouds a good sailor
Even salesmen, their wares still trying to sell,
But not a lawyer, 'cause they're all roasting in hell.

THE REAL TRUTH ABOUT THE BURDEN OF PROOF

I was sitting in the courtroom where justice I would seek,
Had been there a few short hours that seemed more like a week.
"All rise," I heard the bailiff cry, then, "No please take your seat."
The judge, upon the bench, now sat and eyed the docket sheet.
"Who is the lowly wretch who upon my decision now does wait?"
The judge inquired and I stood, prepared to face my fate.
"It is I, Your Honor, and I pray, with me, you'll surely lenient be,
And, perhaps before this day is done, you will have set me free."
"Though it may seem to you the scales of justice are atilt,
Until you prove your innocence to me, I shall presume your guilt."
The judge shouted back in an angry voice like thunder,
"Prove your innocence, or the local jail you'll be under."

STIMULUS ANTHEM!

Oh, say can you see by the morning's light.
The stimulus bill Congress passed under cover of night?
A bill full of wastefulness, earmarks and pork,
To fund politician's pet projects from L.A. to New York.
There's billions for failing corporations and insolvent banks,
Do their CEO's receive it with all good intentions?
No! They throw lavish parties and give themselves high pensions.
And if you've been irresponsible and can't now pay your debt,
You, too, can get in line, to see how much dough you can get.
There's money to build highways leading to nowhere,
But if there's a buck in it for people, they don't seem to care.
And, if from the bill they'll get big bucks, or even a few cents,

What do they care how little is spent for defense?
And they don't seem worried about Congress' fool caper,
Or that Red China now holds most of our nation's paper.
Oh! Say is that greed-spattered banner still wavin'
O'er the land of the freebie and the home of the cravin'?

THE NEW MEXICAN NATIONAL ANTHEM

José, can you see by the dawn's early light
That border we crossed under cover of night?
Across which from the twilight's last gleaming
Aliens by the hundreds were illegally streaming?
While, through their scurrilous flight, bright stars and moon so fair
Gave proof through the night that no sentries were there.
José, does that Mexican flag already wave
O'er this once proud land of the free and home of the brave?

WEEP NO MORE MY LADY

Oh, the Statue of Liberty, she saw it all!
Saw the planes hit and saw the towers fall.
And though Lady Liberty surely wept that day,
She bowed not her head except to pray.
For those who by the cowards' deed did die,
And she still holds her flaming torch on high.
That freedom's light might still brightly glow,
And let all on earth who see it know
That America, to vile aggression, will never yield
And will be, forever freedom's strongest shield.
So weep no more, my lady. Please weep no more
For freedom shall prevail whate'er may be the store'.

THE IRAQ WAR CHRONICLES

2003
We're fighting a war in far-off Iraq.
Some say it's to bring democracy back,
To end Saddam Hussein's despotic reign.
And give the Iraqis their freedom again
Well, it's freed lots of 'em, freed 'em from life,
As they've been killed by bomb, bullet and knife.
Others say it's to end the threat of the WMD,
You know, all those weapons we never did see.
Many, so many, you might call them a legion
Say it's to bring peace to the Middle East region.
Now, that last one I find really quite funny,
Peace among the Shiites, the Kurds and the Sunni?
These rationalizations, I have hated to despoil,
But don't you think this war's really about oil?

2007
The Iraq war is nearly o'er,
The once certain victory surely lost.
Very little, there, did we achieve,
But, oh, how great has been the cost.
Many brave coalition men and women
Were killed and in early graves were laid.
Yet withdrawing our combat troops from Afghanistan
As we did in Iraq is now our nation's current plan
Coming home at last? No, I fear some new hysteria
We'll be sending them all now, instead, to Syria.

BY THE BLOOD OF OTHERS STAINED

In America, our freedom lets us achieve,
But we do it not alone for I believe
That we are not within ourselves alone contained
For we have been by the blood of others stained.

The blood of Jesus who, when nailed on Pilate's tree
Suffered there that we might, from our sins, be free.
The blood of those who dared to sail across the sea
To establish here an English colony

The blood of rebels who once stood against the crown
To form this great nation which they've handed down.
The blood of those who in our nation's wars have fought.
And with their own lives our precious freedom bought.
And who carry high the torch of freedom's light.

So if you think your life is all of your own device
Then you've forgotten these others' sacrifice,
For we are not within ourselves alone contained
And we have been by the blood of others stained.

WOUNDED WORLD

Oh, wounded world, weeping sore,
That man so often wages war.
Politicians send the young out to die
Yet, speak not the true reason why.
Principle has nothing to do with war,
'Tis politics, greed and nothing more.
Oh, wounded world, weeping sore
That man so often wages war.

Oh, wounded world, weeping read
Blood of its children, so many dead,
Sent to war, from childhood, barely freed,
A sacrifice on man's altar of greed.
Their innocent trust, rejected, spurned
That others might have some selfish token earned.
Oh, wounded world, weeping read
Blood of its children, so many dead.

Oh, wounded world, weeping keen
O'er war's destruction, so obscene
What both God and man have created
By man's senseless war is desecrated
And many youth in early graves are lain
That others might some wartime profit gain.
Oh, wounded world, weeping keen
O'er war's destruction, so obscene.

Oh, wounded world, weeping long
While singing mankind's funeral song.
For if man cannot learn to live in peace
And from waging war his efforts cease.
All the gifts God has given man to use,
Man, through senseless war, will surely lose.
Oh, wounded world, weeping long
While singing mankind's funeral song.

DEAD END

Like salty tears fall from a weeping widow's eyes,
Acid rain falls from the earth's dark poison-clouded skies,
That man may bow at the altar of his god, oil
All the green spaces on this earth, man will despoil.

Rhinos, tigers and, yes, even lowly roaches
Die out as man upon their space encroaches.
The deer have little space in which to raise their fawns
Yet man keeps his useless, contaminated lawns.

Global warming's set the polar ice caps a-melt
And it won't be long til its sad effects are felt.
Too many rain forest acres man has stripped bare,
But try to find anybody who seems to care.

Factories and autos spew their polluting smoke
Yet our leaders treat ecology as a joke.
Man's quest for more oil pits brother against brother
For as soon as one war ends, man starts another.

Will many see his folly and try to set it straight?
I fear he'll not and that, alas, it is too late.
That man should rule the earth was, by man, just presumed
And his greed will not end until the earth's consumed.

A PLACE NOW DEAD

A sentient shadow now shields the nurturing sun
From once verdant valleys where rolling rivers rushed to run.
Fields where green grass grew, now brown and barren lie,
'Tis a place where nothing lives and all things there must die.
Those rolling rivers which once ran so pure and blue
Are now silt-laden and as thick as glue,
Not a ray of light can now reach that place,
Only the dreaded darkness now fills its space.
Where is this place that is now so dead?
It's within me, my heart, my soul, my head.
Oh wouldst that I, those rolling rivers could restore,
Or make those brown and barren fields what they were before.
But, alas, my true love has now from me flown,
And I must now pass my way, full alone
Beneath that sentient shadow that now shields the sun,
From once verdant valleys where rolling rivers rushed to run.

To learn more about our other fine books
from Story Arts Media please visit:
www.storyartsmedia.com

An enhanced iBook edition of *Verse or Perverse*
is available for iPad featuring original musical scores
of six of the poems as composed by Benjamin Boone
and performed by pianist Natasha Kislenko
and tenor Randolph Lacey.